Magical Mundane

Poetic reflections on motherhood

holding on and letting go

Snehal Amembal

MAGICAL MUNDANE

Poetic reflections on motherhood - holding on and letting go

Copyright © *Snehal Amembal,* 2025
All Rights Reserved

This book is subject to the condition that no part of this book is to be reproduced, transmitted in any form or means; electronic or mechanical, stored in a retrieval system, photocopied, recorded, scanned, or otherwise. Any of these actions require the proper written permission of the author.

Author Bio

Snehal is a freelance writer and poet based in Surrey (UK). Her writing primarily reflects her motherhood journey, memories of her own childhood and the essence of everyday moments which she tries to document on her blog
Notes On The Go (www.notesonthego.co.uk).
She has authored three poetry chapbooks, 'Pause', 'I Am' and 'In Between Love'. Snehal's debut memoir PapaMa's Portrait is due to be published this year. Snehal is a Young Onset Parkinson's Disease (YOPD) warrior and creates awareness about the condition through her writing. You can find her on Instagram: @notesonthego

To,

Mummy

(for showing me how it's done - well, mostly!)

&

Pappa

(for knowing when to step in and when to step away)

Acknowledgements

I would like to thank my sons Ronak and Rikhil, who continue to make me experience motherhood in all its glory - from the messy to the magnificent. I began writing these poems because of the encouragement from the wonderful folks at Mum Poets Press and Mothership Writers - thank you for your continued love and support. This book would not have been possible without the guidance of Emily and her team at Panda Publishing. Finally, a huge thank you to my husband Rohit - parenting is crazy yet rewarding and there is no one else that I'd do this with!

Contents

Sweet Sleep   1

Teething   2

Wiping   3

Frustrating Friday   4

Toddler Thoughts   5

Restless   6

Imperfections   7

Safe Place   8

Motherhood is.... An Alliteration   9

Midnight Memories   10

Blossoms   11

Learning Through Doing   12

Finding Shapes in Clouds   13

Loose Threads   14

Bubbles   15

Strawberry Kisses   16

First Word   17

I think that I could Never See a Poem as Lovely as.... 18

Everyday Things   19

Bugs   20

Last Day of Preschool   21

Magic	22
Colouring	23
Milestone Miracles	24
Savage September Solitude	25
The Days Grow Short	26
Ronak	27
Rikhil	28
If I Can Stop One Heart from Breaking Let it be Yours	29
Snail	30
River	31
Bittersweet Magic	32
Paper Boat	33
You Grew Up	34
Art	35
I Cannot Tell You	36
It's Been a Long Morning and I'm Craving my First Cuppa Tea	37
How I Do What I Do	38
Sundays	39
Spellbound	40
October Half Term	41
Front Porch Conversations	42
Tiny Version of You	43
Blowing Raspberries	44
Inner Child	45

Reading	46
Why?	47
On Your 1st Birthday	48
Always on The Move	49
Touch of Magic & Mayhem	51
Our Boys and You	52
Happy	53
My Favourite Things Age 4	54
Christmas Eve	55
Sleepy Sojourn	56
Delicate Breath	57
Mealtimes	59
Spider Mother	60
My Sunshine	62
Things I Eat Now that I have a Toddler and Baby	63
Map on my Palms	64
Makeup	65
Motherhood Paradox	66
Patches	67
Ice cream	68
Summer	69
Counting Tiles	70
Comfortable Chaos	71
Five	72

Flamboyant Fall	73
When we told you another baby was coming	74
Lifeboat	75
Light	76
Steps	77
An Ode to Second Borns	78
An Ode to First Borns	79
Stones	80
Portrait of My Sons	81
Mumbai Meandering	82
Crazy In Love	83
What Am I To Do?	84
Morning Pause	85
Transformation	86
What Is Poetry, Mummy?	87

Sweet Sleep

I whisper sweet nothings to you
whilst you stare at me with eyes wide open.
It's way past midnight and
you refuse to go back to sleep.
I rock you gently in my arms,
looking up at the stars for quiet reassurance.
I pace the length of our bedroom,
hoping the motion will soon lull you to sleep.
But you only seem interested in what the night has to bring,
what the moon has to say.
I persist a while longer until I give in to the reality
of our tangled arms upon the bed.
Finally I feel you drifting off to sleep
Your head resting upon my shoulder
Sighing, smiling, peace.

Teething

Milk teeth cutting through gums
Stalactites and stalagmites
Excavation has begun

Wiping

Wiping, wiping, wiping..
Soiled bottoms, Spit ups
Grubby hands and dirty feet.

Wiping, wiping, wiping..
Spilled drinks, scattered snacks
Splashed paint and muddy floors.

Wiping, wiping, wiping..
Rude names, unkind sneers
Fat tears and genuine fears.

Wiping. Wiping. Wiping.

Frustrating Friday

My glass of wine sitting untouched
I will you to sleep
White noise
Nursery rhymes
Silence
Nothing works

Frustrating Friday
I scream internally

I wonder if you heard me because
You climb upon me
Your head resting on my chest
And then slowly sleep closes in

All this while you were seeking to connect
But I did not listen
Exhausted, I sigh
Drifting away with you

Toddler Thoughts

Muddy puddles
Pizza, chips and ice cream
That's MINE!

Dinosaur fights
Paw Patrol, PJ Masks and Peppa Pig
Pretend play is FUN!

The Gruffalo
Parks, Zoos and Farms
Let's go! NOW!

New Potty
Underpants, jumper and jacket
I'll do it by MYSELF!

Bedtime shenanigans
Books, stories and cuddles
I love you Mummy!

Restless

Restless, without rest.

You, me.

Child, mother.

We both need rest

Sleep, relax.

You, me.

When will balance be restored?

Imperfections

Unmade bed, toys strewn around
Messy kitchen, books askew
Laughter, chaos, tight cuddles
Lending perfection
To my perceived imperfections

Safe Place

They say you're often cranky
Throwing tantrums just for me
But what do they know my darling
You feel the safest you'll ever be?

My arms, my lap, my sweet nothings
Caress your worries away
I am your safe place to land my love
After a difficult day

I'm your greatest comfort, my dearest
A place you always seek
So I don't pay heed to what they say
'Cos only you matter to me

Motherhood is.... An Alliteration

Sleepless, Sighs, Sexy, Snacks, Sweetheart, Stop, Songs, Sunrise,
Sunshine, Stars, Shapes, Smoothies
Superpower, Shopping, Shoes, Shit

Silence, Screams, Sand, Sea
Somehow, Stickers, Sprinkles, Shy
Self-reliance, Sugar, Supper, Share
Sippycup, Sanity, Solitude, Support,

Socks, Strawberries, Soul, Stir,
Simplicity, Sniffles, Snails, Sick
Sticks, Sandwiches, Signs, Surprise
Scrunchies, Self-esteem, Smiles

Shadows, Superheroes, Sweets
Sweater, Swears, Shampoo, Slide
Swing, Summer, Scones, Stories
Sorry, Spring, Swift, Survival

Midnight Memories

My waters breaking just past midnight,
Making my way to the hospital.
Anticipation of the process,
Excitement to finally see you.

You making an appearance just before midnight,
Holding you close, my firstborn.
Anticipation of my new role,
Excitement of our journey ahead.

Blossoms

This morning we went for a walk in the woods.
Just you and me after what seemed like ages.
You were enamoured by the way in which the trees embraced each other, by how the wildflowers smiled happily as we sauntered across, by how the sun shined through the foliage as if it were a spotlight.

We spoke about the Gruffalo and his friends.
We also spoke about the Tales of Acornwood
Your voice attained a slight quiver as you were overcome with pure excitement.
You began hunting for bugs and delighted in their appearance.
A squirrel devouring a nut made you squeal in amusement.

We walked some more and suddenly you paused and ran the other way.
Confused, I ran too, calling after you to stop

You eventually stopped where the wildflowers grew and reached out to me with a handful of blossoms.
"These are for you, Mummy"
And just like that you my darling made my day.

Learning Through Doing

You've always been more attracted to blocks, play dough and puzzles
Making, building, creating, doing
You're not one to sit and observe, no
Always on the move, go go go

Climbing on slides the other way round
Conquering the dining table with zealous pride
Trying to swim in the bathtub as if it were the sea
Sprinting up the stairs at the speed of light
Lifting the toy basket with all your might

Doing and learning
Learning and doing
If movement were to be personified
I'm convinced it'd be you!

Finding Shapes in Clouds

Some days when I tire easily
I am thankful for the sky
For I have to lie down to really appreciate its boundless glory

You often lie down next to me
You tell me how blue the sky is and how the clouds drift along slowly
"There's a dog in the sky, Mummy!"
"A triangle is eating cake"
"There's a ginooormus pizza right there Mummy!"
"Where are the clouds going?"
"Look! I can see a car Mummy!"
"Can you see a frog now? It's next to the car…Can you?"

And on and on you go
Finding shapes in clouds
So, some days when I tire easily
I am thankful for the sky.

Loose Threads

I see the loose threads on your jumper

The frayed ends of your jeans

Your T-shirt threatening to fade

Guilt sears deeply through my heart

I remember your brother in these exact same clothes

Before they became hand-me-downs

When they were once privileged enough

to call a wash cycle their own

Then I see you making your own memories

 in these precious pre-loved clothes and my heart gently

mellows

You maybe second born but

never for a moment feel that you are second best

Bubbles

There are days that close in on me
And my mind draws a blank
So I seek out magic in the mundane
"Bubbles" I think, desperately looking for
the magic wand
I feel myself sighing into the wand and the bubbles emerge like
little baubles of hope
Onwards and upwards they rise
Now, you are both squealing in pure delight
Your joy instantly cloaking my sadness with its powerful chime
"More, more, more!" you chant, I happily oblige
The afternoon slowly beginning to take a life of its own

Strawberry Kisses

Food never seemed to interest you
You were always suspicious of it
Never willing to give it a second chance
You would throw it, maul it, squash it within your little fist
almost in anger

I would often get frustrated but wouldn't tire in the hope that
something someday might take your fancy
Something worthy enough of your ever-discerning taste
So one day I kept a whole strawberry in front of you and
feigning disinterest I walked away

The lush red strawberry immediately grabbed your curiosity
You seemed to admire it for a while before biting into it with
your toothless gums
I stood watching you until you finished the whole fruit
I was so pleased that I lifted you up in my arms
And you my darling showered me with sweet strawberry kisses

First Word

Your first word was 'more'
not 'Mummy' not 'Daddy' but 'more'
It is ironic because you have always been a child of few words,
snugly secure in a world of your own.
A world of make-believe where your imagination is boundless,
where I sometimes feel like a stranger
Often you remind me of myself with your sensitive and
thoughtful ways
Perhaps 'more' was after all an apt word
Because my darling the world needs more souls like you

I think that I could Never See a Poem as Lovely as….

(after Joyce Kilmer Trees)

I think that I could never see a poem as lovely as a child's laughter
Where each word pours out so beautifully
It instantly envelopes your heart
Where your inner child is awakened in all its child-like glory
Where innocence is reflected from every syllable creating rhythm
Where you are drawn into their magical world even if for a few seconds
Where you are filled with hope and love
Oh I think that I could never see a poem as lovely as a child's laughter

Everyday Things

Though you may not remember the little everyday things,
You must know that it is these very things that held us together when the tide was high.
The short walks to the park, coco pops for breakfast, reading our favourite books…

When life got overwhelming these everyday things brought some calm.
Loading the washing, making pancakes, listening to our favourite songs
When I felt like giving up I turned to these everyday things to pull me back up.
Bathtime with dinosaurs, hunting for bugs, watching our neighbour's dog bounding across the street…

So even though you may not remember these everyday things
You must know that these were indeed the most special ones.

Bugs

You were always fascinated by bugs
In all their creepy crawly glory
Your voice bubbling with excitement as soon as you spotted one
"Look Mummy look!"
Ladybirds, spiders, ants and worms
"No killing bugs," you admonished your baby brother as he eagerly tried to grasp an ant.

You welcomed all bugs with open arms
So one day we made a bug house
And I was overcome with so much love for you
You asked me if we can make beds, and skipped away looking for leaves
You also asked me about their food and where they'd brush their teeth

It's then that I made a wish
For your love of wilderness to grow with you
And for your innocence to be preserved somewhere deep within the chambers of your precious heart

Last Day of Preschool

Yesterday you graduated from preschool.
Singing "I'm ready to go" at the top of your voice; Your friends and you surprisingly in tune.
As the music played and the sun shone brightly, the atmosphere was buzzing with optimism and excitement.
Suddenly you looked so grown up, with a graduate's hat and gown to match.
A quiet confidence, so sure of yourself, my baby with a clear mind of his own.
And when you strode towards your teacher to collect your graduation certificate;
I remembered my unsteady gait as I pushed your pram through the nursery doors for the first time;
Unsure but hopeful

Magic

It's been a long day
I sit surrounded by what looks like the aftermath of a tornado
Toys, books and crayons lie forgotten on the floor whilst the both of you play tag
Just about avoiding an accident
I speak to you harshly in a tainted tone of voice
"Tidy up, now!"
You continue running oblivious of what has been asked of you
Shrieking in candied delight you run towards me
Landing on my lap with utmost glee
At that moment, I am surrounded by so much love that the mess is instantly forgotten
For you both bring magic to my world

Colouring

I would often do colouring to strengthen my hand; one that had fallen prey to disease
You'd be fascinated by this activity, one that's not really meant for grown-ups
You never mentioned this once
Instead you were always cajoling and encouraging, even reminding me to sit down and colour
"Can I watch you Mummy?" You'd politely ask, sitting next to me
"Would you like to help me choose a colour?" I'd respond with a question
"Yes Mummy! Yes!"
You'd then choose one colour after another
You choosing, me colouring
Me colouring, you choosing
And on and on we'd go
You bringing colour to my dull day

Milestone Miracles

You entered the world, our little miracle of life.
The weeks passed in a blur when suddenly, you smiled the most beatific smile.
Then one day you rolled over, left to right, your bemused expression still fresh in my mind.
We were once reading your favourite book, and you sat up! Me shouting "look, look!"
The days rolled by, we were playing ball and just like that I saw you crawl!
Then came your first steps, a miracle indeed; your first signs of independence through this marvellous deed.
Finally, we heard your very first word, it's only the beginning; more miracles will unfurl.

Savage September Solitude

It's a weekday afternoon
You my precious are at school, exploring a whole new world
Your little brother is fast asleep, exploring his very own dream world
Both worlds are foreign to me, indicating a sort of permanence
You carving your own space within what was once only our special place
A time when you didn't know anyone else but me
This speed of change halts me
I'm not sure if what I feel is lonesome loneliness or a sort of savage September solitude
Whatever it is, I know that I need to embrace it
For the only way now is forward.

The Days Grow Short

The days grow short or so it appears.
My winter babe, you seem to be at peace with autumn's advent.
Is it because it will soon herald the season of your birth?

When night takes over day in the midst of the afternoon
The sun shying away like a newlywed bride;
Leaving the room bereft of her radiance?

When the freezing cold makes its presence felt almost immediately
Our face being bitten when we step into its frosty embrace;
Reminding us perhaps of a lover scorned?

So when you refuse to be bundled up in layers of warm clothing
Or kick away your blanket in the middle of the night
I fret a little less and smile a little more
To see you comforted by the season of your birth.

Ronak

Your name means exuberance, illumination, light.
My eternal sunshine through the darkest of nights.

Your name to me is comfort, thoughtfulness and innocence.
It encapsulates a heart full of love,
a mind so curious.

It's your name I call out when worried or scared
Your name in my prayers, forever, always.

Rikhil

Your name means eternal, forevermore
My infinite strength, of that I'm sure.

Your name to me is generosity, kindness and laughter
Its syllables creating music, love ever after.

I seek out your name in times of despair
Your name on my lips, in my every prayer.

If I Can Stop One Heart from Breaking Let it be Yours

Wrap it in cotton wool so soft that it protects you from every blow.
Strengthen it with twine so strong that it gives you courage forever more.
Make it shine like a mirror anew so that harm is deflected from your very core.

And when you grow up to be a fine young man,
I hope you'll still remember the affectionate little boy whose heart was wrapped in cotton wool, strengthened with twine and shone like a mirror.

Snail

Yesterday you brought home a lone leaf.
"I found it outside my school gate Mummy," you said, a happy smile lighting up your face.
"What's so special about the leaf?" I asked.
"There's a snail on it !" you excitedly announced.
"A snail?"
"Yes Mummy! It was lying there on the leaf all alone so I brought it home," you explained.
"That's very kind of you darling," I said,
My heart bursting at its seams with so much love for you.

You then stepped out into the garden to get some leaves.
"What if it's cold and hungry Mummy?"
Your concern reflecting in your beautiful brown eyes.
Only when you were convinced of the tiny creature's comfort,
Did you move on to playing with your favourite toys.
It is then that I made a wish.
For your love of all creatures to always be your guiding force.
For it is indeed your superpower.

River

The river always helped calm you,
The gentle breeze lulling you to sleep.

As I pushed your buggy along its bank
I felt like Mother Nature was nurturing me to help nurture you.

The river always filled you with joy,
Your tubby feet finding their way towards the water.

As I ran after you to make sure you're safe
I felt like Mother Nature was protecting me to help protect you.

So today, I miss the river and its life-affirming ways
But then, I see vast expanses of green and feel quietly reassured

Bittersweet Magic

Today I was reminded of June 2017.
Something about the way the sun was shining took me back to that day
When I felt an immense need to see you, to hold you.
You, snug in my womb; your arrival wasn't due for another month.

Fast forward 4 years, you my summer baby will start school soon.
The same sun shone brightly today.
So, I held you close, to my heart's content
As we were surrounded by a cloud of bittersweet magic.

Paper Boat

Today I dropped you off at nursery for the very first time.
You, my sweet firstborn were scared and confused.
Who were all these new people?
Your world which only had Mummy and Daddy, expanded overnight.

I could see the fear in your eyes, the sadness on your face.
Guilt tore me apart like a raging bull shredding a red cloth.
I questioned myself, the choices I made.
Somewhere deep inside l knew you would settle soon and you did!

I still remember the day when at drop off you cheerfully waved me goodbye.
My heart bobbing like a paper boat
Sailing unsteadily through another phase of motherhood.

You Grew Up

Somewhere...

Between changing nappies
And night feeds
You grew up

Between first steps
And first words
You grew up

Between fetching water
And fixing snacks
You grew up

Between your first day at nursery
And first day at school
You grew up

Art

I placed a little red
Then a little blue
I could see his mind whirring
Captivated by the hue

He then, placed a little yellow
Then a little green
His mind now entirely curious
What colour had he seen?

I Cannot Tell You

I cannot tell you how deep the sea is
But I can teach you how to swim
I cannot tell you where our stories end
But I can teach you how to begin
I cannot tell you how many books there are
But I can teach you how to read
I cannot tell you why some plants wither
But I can teach you to sow a seed

I may not know the answer to your every question
But together my child, we'll learn
The universe holds wonders aplenty
Come now, it is your turn..

It's Been a Long Morning and I'm Craving my First Cuppa Tea

"Please could you read to him?" I ask.
Knowing well that you can't read, that you are after all merely 3. 3 and a half to be precise.

"Ok Mummy!" you excitedly say, always eager to please. You grab a farm book, your favourite kind and instruct your baby brother, all of 16 months to sit down.

Then slowly the magic happens. "What does the cow say?" you ask. He moos. "What does the horse say?". He neighs. "And the duck?" On and on and on. You ask, he responds, he responds you ask; I am mesmerised by the rhythm.

My cup of tea long forgotten.

How I Do What I Do

Gratitude for my many blessings. My husband, parents, grandmother, kids and bestie. Laughter. Books - for the kids and myself. Good food. The ability to accept change and go with the flow. Physiotherapy. Tea. Making decisions. Music. Setting positive goals. A shower. Fresh air. Determination. Courage. Letting go. Asking for help when necessary. Red wine. Working as a team. Poetry. Writing, always writing.

Sundays

Sundays are made up of hearty breakfasts, leisurely lunches, gardening, DIY, long walks in the park, reading, movies and self-care.

Sundays are also made up of tiresome chores, hurried homework, erratic errands, meal prep, social obligations and the onset of Monday blues.

But, the best Sundays are made up of nothingness.
An oasis in the midst of an arid desert
A fireplace on a cold winter's night
Quite simply, a breath of fresh air

Spellbound

I thought I was prepared, to welcome mini-me
How naive I was, a mother-to-be.
We fought long, we fought hard
For your safe arrival into my arms.

You and me, Me and you.
Push, breathe,
Breathe, push

Then suddenly I saw you in all your magnificent glory!
Your rosy lips, your perfect nose
Your beautiful fingers, your tiny toes
Oh your voice! Your big brown eyes.
I lay there entirely mesmerised.

October Half Term

Every morning we wake up a little later than usual
The night stretching its arms, drawing us back into its embrace
The clocks will soon go back an hour giving us a precious extra sixty minutes
Our days now are filled with playtime and reading
Interspersed with homework for a 4-year-old
The weather has changed and we are all nursing colds
We have Halloween to look forward to so we plan outfits, decorate the house and sing along to spooky rhymes
I allow you cheeky treats for breakfast trying to preserve these precious days of your childhood
Somewhere within the deepest pockets of my treasure trove of memories

Front Porch Conversations

Today we read a book about crayons and colours.
I asked you which one's your favourite
And in a flash you replied "yellow!"
"Because the sun is yellow, Mummy"
You, summer's babe, have always been happiest at its peak.
The sweltering heat does nothing to perturb you.
You don't wilt, you bloom.

As I was gushing over your loveliness you asked me if you could colour and went on to bring some paper and a purple crayon.
"Today I'll colour the sun purple, Mummy."
"Oh! Why purple?" I asked confused.
"Because I can," you said simply.
Our front porch conversation leaving me entirely amazed.

Tiny Version of You

It's only a matter of days until you'll outgrow my lap.
I will miss this version of you, just like I miss that of your older brother.
Your long eyelashes, soft like feathers on the back of a newly hatched fledgling.
Your lips, pink like rosebuds, pouting in response to the sun's first rays.
Your breathing, gentle like the rise and fall of waves in a calm sea.
So I let you lie on my lap for longer than I intend to, savouring each moment that seems to be slipping away from my fingers;
Slowly at first then with immense speed, reminding me of desert sand.

Blowing Raspberries

Early morning kisses;
Blowing raspberries on your tummy
As you burst into a gale of giggles.
I trace the pillowy soft folds of your arm
As you try to wriggle away in glee.
Outside, dawn is just breaking.
The first rays of the sun stream in,
Lending a golden halo to your cherubic face.
In that moment I am grateful, so grateful for you, this moment,
us.

Inner Child

I often become wordless in the wilderness
when the child within me emerges.
She is in awe of nature's magic;
Of how the butterflies appear so beautifully from their cocoon
The spots on a ladybird, their delicate details, the colours
perfectly in contrast
Of how the fuzzy petals of a dandelion fly away even with the
lightest whiff of air
The river determining its own path through the trickiest of
bedrock
And when her heart is full of nature's glory
She promises herself to learn from its pace- patient,
perseverant, quietly powerful.

Reading

"Mm-uh-mm," Dd-ae-dd
The sounds roll off your tongue
The resulting words seem foreign when pronounced like that
"I can connect them in my brain Mummy, Mrs Potter showed me how," you tell me excitedly
I am equally excited for you to learn this skill that will educate you yes but more than that
For it to lead you into the magical world of books
A world of your own where you choose what to experience through the beauty of words
So I sit beside you and watch you read
My heart swelling with pride
Wondering how soon we got here

Why?

Why is the sky so high Mummy
Where do ants sleep
Why does a cat have four legs Mummy
Are there more cows than sheep

Why is the sun so hot Mummy
How do bugs talk
Why should I brush my teeth Mummy
Who lives under that rock

Why can't I eat 50 chocolates Mummy
Does the moon not sleep at all
Why does the rainbow have so many colours Mummy
Is the earth as big as my football?

You ask me all these questions
With one hand under your chin
I want to capture your sense of wonder
So that it's never ever ruined

On Your 1st Birthday

To love someone so deeply
A love unconditional and pure
A love that many have spoken of
To cherish, hold close, secure…

To be your mother's a privilege
A bond so resilient and strong
I'll hold you now in my arms
And sing to you your favourite song…

For I know you'll grow up too quickly
Some long days now, they'll disappear
And when morning comes one fateful day
It's you that I'd want to find near…

But you'd have flown our loving nest
To make one of your own
However tightly I want to hold on now
I will eventually have to let go…

So as you turn one my dear son
I wish you every success and joy
Whatever you do, wherever you go,
To me, you'll still be my little boy.

Always on The Move

"Mummy whatchaa wearing Mummy?"
You ask, As you see my new hairband
I burst out laughing at this question asked to me by a nearly 2-year-old
You then run away squealing in delight
Leaving me utterly impressed by your keen sense of observation and eloquence
But I don't have too much time to ponder over this
As I run after you to make sure you're safe
The need to protect you always kicking in

You rest a while by the dining table distracted by a colourful steel tumbler
You pick it up, pretend to drink from it then fling it at the floor while it drips off
Clang clang clang
You clap your hands, delighting in the act
I sternly ask you to stop
But again, you run away squealing in delight
And I run after you to make sure you're safe
The need to protect you always kicking in

It's only when you sleep that I catch my breath
Your angelic face lending you a sense of innocent vulnerability
I sit beside you to make sure you're safe
The need to protect you always kicking in

Touch of Magic & Mayhem

Mornings are manic
Yet strangely mellifluous
In our home
Where innocent souls
Run amok
Without a care in the world

Laughter bouncing
off the walls
"Mummmmyyyyy"
A war cry of sorts
Breathe in, breathe out
"Mmmmmm mangoes"

I close my eyes
Trying to picture you both
As toddlers
Memory miserably failing
I revel in the now
This magical mayhem

Our Boys and You

Pulling me close when I push you away
Our boys and you on a warm summer's day
Doing the dishes, sorting the bins
Listening to me patiently
Talking nonsense things

Wishing me good morning, that hot cuppa tea
You making oats porridge so diligently
Dropping our boys, rushing to work
Working harder than ever
Complaining? No. Never

Love takes on many guises, as life goes on
With Our boys and you Im never forlorn
You are my strength, my one and only
With you by my side
Even a dark day seems sunny

I could go on, there's so much to say
Your love me shines through in every way
Wherever you go, only mine you will be
Our boys and you
And you and me

Happy

Your father and I were rushing around to get us all ready and out of the house
Your brother and you were chasing each other from room to room
Entirely ignoring our requests to "stop, hurry up and get changed."
Even threats of Santa putting you on the naughty list failed to work
So we decided to be quiet for a moment as we considered our next move

Thank While we were contemplating this, we heard your voice, hesitant yet strangely confident
"Huh, ae puh puh…..Happy! Happy!"
You my darling had just read a word from my T-shirt!
Your father and I immediately looked at each other with a hint of disbelief yet brimming with pride

I wonder if you'll remember what happened next
Your Mummy jumping up and down
Saying, "He can read! He can read! He can read a big word!"
And just like that you won us over
Lending us perspective on what really matters

My Favourite Things Age 4

New books to read and bugs to explore
Chocolate and candy and superheroes
Snacks that are really fit for a king
These are a few of my favourite things

Playing with Rikhil and dinosaur fights
My swimming lessons and Christmas lights
Songs in the bathroom that I love to sing
These are a few of my favourite things

Going to school and friends' birthday parties
Weekly Cricket coaching and saying "Me Hearties"
All cats and dogs, the joy they do bring
These are a few of my favourite things

When Amamma leaves
When Mummy screams
When I'm feeling sad
I simply remember my favourite things and then I don't feel so bad!!

Christmas Eve

"Jingle bells! Jingle bells! Alethaaa play Jingle bells!"
I hear your two-year-old voice commanding Alexa to play your current favourite song.
Your brother is working hard at a jigsaw puzzle and says, "Not againnnn!!".
Your father is busy sorting out some long pending DIY tasks and is rather oblivious of what's happening around him.
Tomorrow is Christmas and we are all looking forward to Santa's visit.
That one day where I wish his magic worked on me too.
"Tanta Claus, Tanta Claus," you shout out as if reading my mind.
Alexa has finally obliged so I lift you up in my arms and together we dance.
Me, desperately trying to preserve this moment,
To help me revel in the pure innocence of childhood.

Sleepy Sojourn

You curl up in my arms
Your head nestled within the nape of my neck
I breathe in your baby smell
As it relieves my tiredness

Your breathing is steady
Its rise and fall slowly lulling me into sweet slumber
I trace the outline of your dimpled cheek
Your lips like rosebuds gently open and close
They reveal bubbles of spittle
And for a moment I am reminded of a mouthful of pearls

I close my eyes and accompany you on your sleepy sojourn
Wondering whether I will get a glimpse into your dreams

Delicate Breath

Those early days of motherhood are seared into my memory
For they were incredibly beautiful and immensely raw

I remember watching your breath like a hawk when you slept peacefully in your cot
Inhale Exhale

I remember holding my fingers under your nose just to be a hundred percent sure
Inhale Exhale

I remember the delicate feel of your soft breath against the nape of my neck
Inhale Exhale

I remember the endless nights of a blocked nose playing havoc with your breath
Inhale Exhale

I remember sitting next to you, counting, counting, counting
Inhale Exhale

So today when your curious four year old self asked me what the lungs do it took me back to those early days
But all I said to you was "Breathe, they help you breathe".

Mealtimes

Mealtimes are mostly manic.
Every morsel meandering around little mouths.
More miming, less chewing.
Messy mess mess!

Marmite, meat or mango?
Macaroni, muesli or melon?
Marvelling at the marble cake?
More more more!

Making memories are we?
Masking mushrooms and mung beans.
Mixing and mashing, muscles emerging?
Mummy Mummy Mummy!

Mmmmmm
Mealtimes are sometimes mellifluous.
Mouths full and hearts fuller.
Magic magic magic!

Spider Mother

I was happily busy spinning my web
for you my dearest firstborn
Always wondering to myself about where the day had gone
Busy busy busy
Spin spin spin

I would feed you and protect you in the only way I knew
A way that so magically
seemed to work for you
Busy busy busy
Spin spin spin

Then along came your little brother
I had to unlearn whatever I knew
My web in apparent disarray
Oh whatever should I do
Busy busy busy
Spin spin spin

My methods weren't working
I was stressed beyond belief
Whatever I did, however much
There wasn't any sign of relief
Busy busy busy
Spin spin spin

Slowly then I learnt his ways
And spun my web differently
Learning new ways on the go
To look after you both confidently
Busy busy busy
Spin spin spin

My Sunshine

It's so easy to doubt myself

When the minutiae of our everyday overwhelms

Am I doing enough? Could I have done better? What if I was fully able?

What if I was fully able?

What if I was fully able?

Such questions haunt me all day long

Sometimes they scare me

At other times they scar me.

Then slowly winter sneaks out the kitchen door

And I begin to hear about the goodness that you exude, the way you light up the room when you walk in

Just like your name, Ronak

And I feel hopeful and optimistic

As Spring gently makes her presence felt.

Things I Eat Now that I have a Toddler and Baby

Sorry looking fruit purées, with a baby spoon

Two-minute noodles standing by the sink

Oat bars have slowly become my go-to food on days that seem to pass in a blur
Soggy cereal soaking in milk, reminding me of long luxurious baths

Pizza crusts dipped in carefully preserved garlic butter pots

A buffet of scrambled eggs, toast, brioche, yoghurt, banana - all of which were deeply desired but ruthless rejected

Consuming chocolate and guilt in equal measure. The same chocolate I refused my toddler an hour ago.

Map on my Palms

I wonder if the map on my palm has your name written on it.
Does it show in its intricacies that I was destined to be your mother?
That your beautiful soul would one day be known as being part of mine?
I also wonder whether this map holds directions for this journey of motherhood.
Are there maps for each child that I birth?
Do they hold secrets to navigating the sometimes confusing pathways that motherhood inevitably brings?
I stare at my palm, then stare at you
I wonder what adventures await us
I then place your palms upon my lap
And make a mother's wish that your map be perfect in every way.

Makeup

"What is this Mummy?" you ask me, holding my pink lipstick in your little hand
"It's lipstick, child," I explain to you, "it's for grownups only".
"Please, can you keep it back in its place?" I request you gently.
You look up at me, a million questions seem to be whirring around in your head.
The lipstick stares smugly at me from your curious hand.
"Can children use it Mummy?" you ask innocently.
"It's only for grownups," I repeat, a slight irritation creeping up into my voice.
You now begin to fiddle with the lipstick, rotating it in and out of its case.
"Stop that!" I shout in annoyance, afraid that you will destroy my prized possession.
You stare at me defiantly and I walk out of the room,
In the hope that diffusing the situation might help.
I impatiently let a few minutes pass and come back to see you standing in front of the mirror,
Your mouth smeared with my favourite hue.
You look at me and I burst out laughing,
Your innocence winning me over, yet again!

Motherhood Paradox

Motherhood a paradox
A melting pot of emotions
A sixth sense so strong
A need to protect, always

A melting pot of emotions
Stirring does not help
A need to protect, always
Preempt, perceive, process

Stirring does not help
Let things be
Preempt, perceive, process
Life goes on

Let things be
Appreciate the pace of nature
Life goes on
Motherhood a paradox

Patches

Images of you float in my mind
You as a newborn, at 6 months old,
18 months, 8 months, 3 yrs, 2.5 yrs
I try to remember what you were like at each of these ages
But my memory robs me of the finer details

I remember your toothless smile but can't remember how many teeth you had at 8 months
I remember your distressed cries but can't remember what helped calm you at 3 months
I remember the day you took your first steps but can't remember when you began running around the house
What was your first full sentence? What was your favourite nursery rhyme at 3? What set you off in a fit of laughter?

You seem to appear in patches when I desperately desire these details
It makes me sad that I will never get to revisit these past versions of yourself
So I hold on tight to whatever I can and foolishly try to immortalise you in the safe embrace of my words

Ice cream

I see you both sitting in the sunshine
Rosy cheeks, icecream in hand
Your gaze upon the icecream is steady
Ensuring it doesn't slide off the cone
I sit and stare at you both
My heart brimming with love
Gratitude emerging in waves
for this moment of quiet calm amidst
the crazy chaos of motherhood

Summer

Summer's here again

Ice Cream rivulets gather

The years melt away

Counting Tiles

22 tiles

22 tiles in our kitchen

The coincidence unnerves me

22nd was your due date

Would you have eaten better if you were a full-term baby?

I am trying to entice you with colourful pasta

You seem least interested in the whole affair

We spend hours in the kitchen, you at the table, me standing beside you, always hopeful

I continue counting tiles, 22 again

I sometimes get distracted by photographs of other children of family and friends eating well, eating more than you, some younger, some older

I question myself- Am I doing enough? Am I doing something wrong? Am I failing as your mother to fulfil your basic need?

Back to counting tiles, still 22

You finally decide to reject the pasta and ask for chapati

You then half-heartedly go on to finish one chapati

I have learnt to accept this as a small win.

22 tiles. I seek comfort in this predictability.

Comfortable Chaos

I begin my day with morning chores.
The reassuring sounds of the kitchen appliances take the sting out
of the sleepless night just gone by.

The two of you begin chasing each other, screaming like
banshees up and down the stairs.
You hurl questions at me as you continue your chase,
interspersed obviously with complaints.
"Where are the crayons?"
"He hit me first."

And before I respond, there is crying, shouting, throwing, screaming
Also laughing, tickling and rolling in glee.

I'm calm amidst this noise,
 so unlike my younger self.
Boldly embracing, confidently thriving,
gladly welcoming, this comfortable chaos.

Five

How did we get here so quickly?
Where did those long days go?
The memories come gushing
 At breakneck speed

I try to pluck out snapshots from your early years
Trying to remember exactly how you looked, what you did,
how you communicated with me
But I fail to pinpoint the details
These details have somehow merged into my memory so
strongly that they refuse to stand apart from each other
 Like grains of overcooked rice

You as a newborn, an infant, a toddler
Now, a little boy
Full of curious charm and kindness
Always protecting your little brother with a cloak of
unconditional love
He Is lucky to have you
We are lucky to have you
You, our firstborn
Always Holding the first sunlight
In your twinkling eyes

Flamboyant Fall

Outside the leaves fall upon the ground
Shades of auburn, brown, red and green
They remind me of a blanket covering the Earth Preparing her for winter's advent
Winter who is not as glamorous as her predecessor the flamboyant Fall

And as nature orchestrates this drama..

You snuggle up on my chest reminding me of those early days where you would sleep there for hours together
You, my winter baby.
So whenever Fall waves her magic wand around
I always remember the last trimester before you entered this world
Bringing much colour to an otherwise dark winter .

When we told you another baby was coming
(After Clint Smith)

When we told you another baby was coming, you were barely 2 years old yourself
You looked at us with your dandelion eyes,
from your dad to me, from me to your dad,
"You are going to become a big brother in December" your dad kindly explained
He held my tummy and said to you, "There's a baby in there!"
"Baby in Sember," you cautiously said, the words tumbling out of your mouth like jellybeans
"He spoke a full sentence!" I exclaimed
Reaching out to your tiny self across my bump
holding you both close to me
And just as I was coming out of this reverie
I was pulled right back in by your Dad's warm embrace
Enveloping us all like a safety net

Lifeboat

"Mummy, Mummy, Mummy"
You never tire of me
Always holding onto me
Hoping I'll save you
Like a lifeboat in tumultuous waters
Unconditional love surrounds me
Your innocence enamouring me
Hoping you'll remain like this
My most precious treasure
Your pain torments me
Your tears stinging my soul
Making you believe in miracles
However morose the morning
And in the middle of the night
When you prise my sleep away
I gather you in my arms
And feel the weight of the day slowly
Leaving my body

Light

If the sun doesn't rise tomorrow remember to shine your light
Let it shine so bright that luminescence envelopes your being
Much like your bright-coloured clogs on a dark gloomy day

A light is always burning deep within you
Do all you can to keep it alive
And on days when you cannot find it

Create your own

Create your own

Create your own

Steps

Guilt rips my heart apart
Watching you both grow up so soon
Thinking always about me your mother

My steps faltering
I watch you watching me now
"Can you walk, Mummy?"

An Ode to Second Borns

Those who complete us, make us whole
I thank you for
Rekindling the abundant love in my heart for you and your older sibling/Awakening gentle appreciation for the pace of nature and the beauty of time/Granting grace for when I am exhausted and spent/Giggling gladly, warming up the cockles of my heart, carry on…I do /Pushing my boundaries and reigning me back in/Looking at me with trusting eyes/Teaching me patience, a lofty virtue/Humouring me as I revel in all your firsts. Your firsts, they are my lasts.

Second born you are but second best you'll never be.

An Ode to First Borns

Those who transform us, allow us our mistakes
I thank you for
Parting with patience as I learn how to nurture both you and your baby sibling/Giving grace when you have to share my attention with other little people/Happily helping with cumbersome chores/Redefining routine and repetition unknowingly saving me time/Asking me if I'm alright in the midst of a chaotic day, trying to do too much at once/Doing everything on your own, the other day you asked me what independence is/Delighting in our impromptu dances, moving me from within/Forgiving faultlessly, smiling ever so sweetly/Energising enthusiasm never failing to add sparkle to an otherwise monotonous day.

Firstborn you are, forever you will be.

Stones

I see you
bending down
collecting another stone

Round, flat, jagged, smooth;
your collection
keeps growing

You always
pick one
from your treasure box

Holding on to it
with all your
two-year-old might

You take it along
on your
little adventures

Seeking quiet reassurance
from this precious piece
of Mother Earth.

Portrait of My Sons

The both of you sit colouring,
Black and white pictures coming to life
Each colour gently caressing your canvas

Blue, red, orange, brown,
black, yellow, green
and purple
of course!

Your brother is cautious, colouring within the lines
You less so, proudly scribbling all over the place
"Look what I made," your brother calls out to me
"Wow!" I say genuinely impressed
"Look what I made", you are quick to follow
"Look what ME made," you change the sentence just in case it
makes a difference to my opinion

"Beaaauuuutiful" I shower praise upon you, my creation
And as you continue to create a collage of colour
I am almost scared to break this sense of surreal space
Making room for your imagination
Uninhibited, boundless, free
Somehow adding magic to the mundane

Mumbai Meandering

Languid summer days
A bagful of memories
Souls brimming with love

Our hearts are so full
Food satiates our being
Four generations

Sweet jasmine ignites
Latent memories emerge
I am mesmerised

Time and space merging
Bound by divine rituals
Immense gratitude

Two sides of a coin
Love and loss coexisting
Life always goes on

Crazy In Love

You stood there
Your seven-year-old self
Wrapped up in a tuxedo
Ready to charm the world

In bounded your little brother
A five-year-old whirlwind of a tuxedo
Forcing me to break my gaze

"Tada!" he screeched
You hugged him tight
And began jumping up and down
In joyous glee

Your dad and I became an audience
Until you pulled us in
And we danced!
To 'Crazy In Love'

"We made them!" I exclaimed
"We sure did!" your dad echoed
He embraced me
And we danced some more

What Am I To Do?

I opened the door to our flat
A loud silence welcomed me
No parking your buggy, no picking you up
No settling you onto the playmat
No juice nor snacks

Your first day at nursery
Was harder than I imagined
Your toys and books staring morbidly
Colourful blocks of lego seeming so meaningless\
As they lay strewn upon the floor
Waiting once again for your little hands
To pick them up

"What AM I to do?"
I thought to myself
The silence almost murderous in its presence
All I did was crash into the sofa
Allowing fat hot tears to soak into all this time that was now
suddenly only mine

Morning Pause

You bound into our bedroom
Your brother and you
Jumping in between your father and me
Making our bed even more cozy

"I'm cold," you say in the midst of summer
I don't argue and give you a tight cuddle
"Me too," your brother says.
 I reach out to him and pull him closer.
We then feel your father's arm landing across us
Loving, protecting, pause.

And as we lie there
The four of us, on our bed
I am thankful, I'm grateful
For this moment, for us.

Transformation

Sometimes I stare at you and wonder.
Whether I birthed you or you, me.

What Is Poetry, Mummy?

"What is poetry Mummy?" you asked me today when I was furiously typing away on my phone.
I was lost for words then but now I attempt to hold onto them, draw them in together and make a coherent whole.
I do this to explain to you what Poetry actually is, what it means.

Poetry is like your toy box holding a variety of toys some that you really like others not so much
But play with them all? You do!

Poetry is you riding your bike, the wind carelessly rustling your soft hair, leaving your delicate cheeks rosy pink.

Poetry is like when you feel really hungry and end up eating a lot of food
Do you eat again tomorrow? You do!

Poetry is you singing your favourite song, playing your favourite game, colouring your favourite pictures

Poetry is like a rainbow, its colours lending hope to an otherwise dreary afternoon.

Poetry is you laughing joyously, your innocence creating a magical bubble, one that I'm afraid to burst.

Poetry is like magic where your feelings become words, those words then come to life and you are left wondering, "But how?"

www.ingramcontent.com/pod-product-compliance
Lightning Source LLC
Chambersburg PA
CBHW060501080526
44584CB00015B/1513